MADE IN AMERICA

H. ROSS
PEROT
Texas Billionaire

Gene Brown

ROURKE ENTERPRISES, INC.
VERO BEACH, FLORIDA 32964

© 1993 Rourke Enterprises, Inc.

All rights reserved. No part of this book may be reproduced or utilized in any form or by any means, electronic or mechanical including photocopying, recording, or by any information storage and retrieval system without permission in writing from the publisher.

A Blackbirch Graphics Book.

Library of Congress Cataloging-in-Publication Data

Brown, Gene.
   H. Ross Perot / Gene Brown.
     p. cm. — (Made in America)
   Includes index.
   Summary: Examines the life and political activities of the wealthy businessman who decided to save America by running for president.
     ISBN 0-86592-060-5
     1. Perot, H. Ross, 1930–   —Juvenile literature. 2. Presidential candidates—United States—Biography—Juvenile literature. [1. Perot, H. Ross, 1930–   . 2. Presidential candidates. 3. Businessmen.] I. Title. II. Series.
E840.8.P427B76   1993
937.928'092—dc20
[B]   93-11998
                                                                     CIP
                                                                     AC

Contents

Chapter 1	**Beginnings**		**5**
	Growing Up in Texarkana		7
	The Naval Academy		9
	An Important Meeting		11
Chapter 2	**Becoming a Billionaire**		**12**
	Dissatisfaction with IBM		14
	Striking Out on His Own		15
	A Golden Opportunity		16
	Life as a Rich Man		18
Chapter 3	**Ross Perot vs. Roger Smith**		**19**
	GM Wins Over Ross		20
	A Big Mistake		23
	Here We Go Again!		26
Chapter 4	**In the Public Eye**		**27**
	A Texan in Washington		27
	A Hero		29
	Ross Helps Texas		30
	POWs and MIAs		31
Chapter 5	**The Biggest Job of All**		**34**
	The "Unofficial" Candidate		34
	The Problems Begin		37
	Ross Returns		41
	An Opportunity Seized		42
	A Force to Be Reckoned With		45
	Glossary		**46**
	For Further Reading		**46**
	Index		**47**

1

Beginnings

"The way to deal with problems is to 'go straight to the top.'"

In 1992, billionaire Ross Perot, challenged the American political system with his unexpected bid for the U.S. presidency. He based his campaign on the motto: "It's time for a candidate who will get down to business."

Ross, running as an independent, said that Americans should vote for him because he knew how to get things done. The proof was his success in business, which had made him one of the world's richest people. As a businessperson, he believed in plain talk. He was used to searching for the best ideas, finding the right people, and moving

Opposite: Ross Perot has lived his entire life with a "can-do" spirit. In the 1992 presidential election, he reshaped American politics with his special brand of determination.

on to other things. He said that made for good business, and it would make for good government. This no-nonsense approach would clean up what he called "the mess" in Washington.

Ross saw life as full of opportunities. But you had to take them—you had to act.

Many Americans were attracted to what Ross said. They could easily relate to Ross and his ideas. Americans liked the idea that Ross did things his own way. He was a rich man who seemed to live a simple life. His wealth and many of his ideas made him a conservative (someone who favors "traditional" ideas). He talked about the importance of "family values," just like President Bush. But Ross often took positions that surprised people. He did not, for example, approve of the Persian Gulf War against Iraq. And he did support a woman's right to choose an abortion. But Americans liked Ross for another reason, too—Ross didn't brag about his years in public office. He didn't have any. Ross emerged at a time when the United States was fed up with "politics as usual." Ross was different.

Where did this man come from? How had he become so wealthy? What made him the way he was?

Growing Up in Texarkana

It's not surprising that Ross Perot should seem so independent and stand for many things that don't ordinarily fit together. He came from Texas, a state where independence has always been important. And his hometown is made up of two parts that were put together from two different states.

Texarkana is on the Texas-Arkansas border. Half the town is in one state, half is in the other. Henry Ray ("Ross") Perot was born in a brick bungalow in the Texas half on June 27, 1930.

While Ross likes to tell people about his modest start, his family appears to have had money. His father, Gabriel Ross ("G. R."), sold horses and traded in cotton.

An earlier child, named Gabriel Ross for his father, had died. Out of respect for his memory, the Perot's didn't want to name their next son Gabriel Ross. They named him Henry Ray. But Mr. Perot still wanted a son named after him. So, when Henry Ray was 12, he had his middle name legally changed to Ross. He did keep his first name, but he has been called either Ross or H. Ross ever since.

Ross says that from his mother, Lulu Ray, he learned to respect and appreciate everyone, even a homeless person on the street. From his father, he got the sense of humor that would later help him in public life. G.R. Perot's cotton business had a sign outside that read, "Sell it. You can't eat it."

Young Ross got a working introduction to the horse business at age eight. That's when his father put him on a horse to break it in. The boy was up to the challenge, but it meant getting thrown off more than once. Still, he just kept getting back on.

Ross attended the only private school in town. Mary Patterson, who ran it, was strict and demanded a lot from her pupils. She taught them dancing along with the traditional academic subjects. They had to dance every week in front of their parents. This got them used to performing in public. Being able to perform before audiences has helped Ross throughout his life.

When he was 12, Ross joined the Boy Scouts. Here he showed that he was willing to work hard for whatever he wanted. Not even one out of a hundred boys in scouting makes the rank of Eagle Scout. But Ross did, in no time at all.

Ross also had a paper route. It took him into some of the roughest parts of Texarkana. Ross rode horseback while he

Growing up in Texarkana during the 1940s, Ross learned responsibility by working as a paper-delivery person, making his deliveries on horseback.

delivered the newspapers. One time, the man in charge of deliveries did not pay Ross what he had coming to him. Ross went over his head to the paper's publisher. It worked. Afterward, Ross said that this had taught him that the way to deal with problems is to "go straight to the top."

The Naval Academy

After studying at Texarkana Junior College, Ross entered the U.S. Naval Academy at Annapolis, Maryland. He wasn't the best student there, but no one at the academy worked harder than he did. Ross became president of his senior class and the head of the honor committee. While a senior, he met Margot Birmingham on a blind date. He later married her in 1956.

Upon graduation in 1953, Ross began his required tour of naval duty. At the time, the United States was at war in Korea, and there was a chance Ross would see action. But the destroyer to which he had been assigned was halfway across the Pacific Ocean, headed for Korea, when the war finally ended.

Young Ross, age 17, poses for a casual shot in 1947.

In 1953, Ross graduated from the U.S. Naval Academy in Annapolis, Maryland. He is shown here in a portrait taken for the academy's 1953 yearbook.

An Important Meeting

What is not in doubt is the effect on Ross Perot of a visitor aboard the *U.S.S. Leyte*, the aircraft carrier that he later served on. The visitor was a salesperson from IBM (International Business Machines). At this time, computers were still new, but there was one on Ross's ship. The man from IBM liked Ross and told him that he would make a good IBM salesperson. That meeting would change Ross Perot's life.

2

Becoming a Billionaire

"Ross Perot...was willing to take risks."

Just out of the navy and recently married, Ross went to work for IBM in Dallas in 1956. The computer business was different from what it is today. There were no personal computers. All of IBM's machines were quite big and expensive. Only the largest companies and the government could afford them.

But IBM was on its way to becoming one of the world's biggest companies, and computer sales were driving its growth. The company was very strict about how its employees should dress and act. Dark suits, white shirts, and conservative ties made up the IBM uniform. And the employees who wore it were expected to be just as conservative in their behavior. That was fine with Ross Perot. Ross liked the atmosphere.

He also liked the fact that IBM had a practice of generously rewarding good work. Ross plunged into the job of selling computers. Because he worked on commission—money paid for selling products—his hard work enabled him to make a lot of money in a short period of time.

After finishing his service in the U.S. Navy, Ross got a job selling computers for IBM. This was his introduction to the world of computers and the beginning of the success that was to come.

Dissatisfaction with IBM

Ross might have continued with IBM as one of its top salespeople. But in 1962, the company began to limit the amount of money any salesperson could make from commissions. This angered Ross. He felt that the only limit on pay ought to be how good a job a person did.

There was also another side of IBM that bothered Ross. Like many big companies, IBM was slow to change. It was difficult to get anyone to listen to new ideas. There was less interest in creativity than in following the rules. To someone like Ross Perot, who often saw different ways of doing things, this was frustrating.

One thing Ross wanted to change was the relationship of IBM to its customers. The company only sold its machines and serviced them. It did very little to help the customers use their new computers to solve problems.

Here, Ross thought, was a big market to be tapped. IBM, or someone, ought to be creating software to go with the computers. Designers could work with consumers to match software to specific jobs.

If IBM wouldn't do it, Ross decided that he would. It was a chance to get in on the ground floor of an important new industry: computer services. Ross required little money to start his business. He just needed a good idea, a willingness to take a risk and work hard, the ability to hire good people to work for him—and a little luck.

Striking Out on His Own

On June 27, 1962, Ross Perot established Electronic Data Systems (EDS). The dress code and the behavior expected of everyone were just like at IBM. But the big difference was that Ross encouraged people to come up with new ideas. And pay was based on how well each person did his or her job.

Unlike the giant IBM, Ross's company was small and flexible. It could change with the times and easily take advantage of new opportunities. Ross Perot, its chief, was willing to take risks. He was always looking for areas of business that other people hadn't gotten into yet, so he might establish himself there first.

Ross hired people like himself for major jobs at EDS. Top employees received shares in the company so that they felt a direct interest in its success. If they did a good job, the company would do well, and they would get part of the profits.

People who go into business have to be resourceful, especially when they first get started and have little money. Ross was up to the task. To save money, EDS rented machines at night from companies that used them only during the day. This helped build the company up without drowning it in expenses.

A Golden Opportunity

In 1965, the U.S. Congress created new programs, Medicare and Medicaid, to help older people and people with low incomes pay their medical bills. The states handled most of the programs, with part of the money coming from Washington.

The new laws helped many people, but they also created big problems for states. State governments found themselves drowning in paperwork. Texas hired Blue Cross–Blue Shield, a private insurance company, to help. But it, too, quickly fell behind.

Ross, who was working part-time for Blue Cross–Blue Shield, saw this as an excellent opportunity for EDS. His company took over the processing of insurance claims. It did the job well and soon got contracts to do the same for other states.

Ross holds up a new piece of computer equipment that was produced by his company—EDS—around 1968. This product replaced the larger model in the background.

EDS got bigger. So did the income of many of its top employees. A hundred of them became millionaires. And their boss was on his way to becoming one of the wealthiest people in America.

By the late 1960s, shares of stock in companies like EDS were rapidly increasing in value. It seemed like a good time to make EDS a public company—to sell shares, allowing many people to own part of it. Ross did this on September 12, 1968. The move was successful beyond his wildest dreams. So many people wanted shares that within a year Ross became a billionaire.

Life as a Rich Man

For the most part, Ross didn't let his new wealth affect his life-style. He bought jewelry for his wife and boats for himself but otherwise lived like someone who was merely comfortable. He was especially careful to make sure that the money didn't spoil his children. He taught them to be thrifty, just as his father had done.

Ross set up a foundation to give away millions of dollars to help pay for hospitals, schools, and other causes. He was also known to be very generous to his friends and employees.

But the picture wasn't all positive. Ross also became known for holding grudges and for becoming angry with anyone whom he felt had "crossed him." Even though Ross placed a high value on loyalty in friends and those working for him, some people questioned whether he always showed the same quality himself. When some of the workers at his California operation started to form a union, for example, Ross closed down his office in that state.

This negative side of Ross Perot was to receive more attention as the man from Texarkana began to live more and more in the public eye.

3

Ross Perot vs. Roger Smith

"Ross was used to making quick decisions, keeping on top of everything."

"I came from an environment where, if you see a snake, you kill it," Ross has remarked. Whenever he sees a problem, he attacks it quickly and directly and then moves on to something else. Most of all, he doesn't want to waste time standing around talking about it.

This kind of attitude made it impossible for him to stay at a big company like IBM. There, any ideas and suggestions had to be reviewed by a committee, then another committee, and so on. Things moved too slowly. It was the way large companies usually do business. It couldn't be more different from the way people like Ross Perot prefer to do things.

Given Ross's style, joining another big company was probably the last thing the billionaire should have done. But in 1984 he did it. And it proved to be a taxing mistake.

GM Wins Over Ross

By the mid-1980s, EDS had become one of America's most successful companies. It was known for using computers to increase the ability of organizations to work better and faster. This brought EDS to the attention of General Motors (GM), the giant car company. GM needed this kind of help.

Through the 1960s, American cars and the companies that made them were on top all over the world. The success of GM, manufacturer of Chevrolets, Buicks, and other models, was one reason for this.

But in the 1970s, Japanese and German cars became more popular, even in America. They were well made, and they were built more quickly and cheaply than American cars. Car buyers were beginning to complain that the quality of American cars had dropped. By the 1980s, foreign cars were crowding out American models.

After selling his share of General Motors stock for a reported $700 million, Ross met with GM executives in Washington, D.C. to discuss the final details of the agreement.

The chairman of GM, Roger Smith, decided that to respond to this challenge, his company needed "automation"—the use of devices, such as computers, to replace the work of people. It would reduce the cost of making cars and the time it took to produce them.

GM did not want to develop automation systems itself. It wanted to buy a company that could do it for them. In the early 1980s, many large companies of all kinds were buying smaller companies. Often they paid large sums of money for them. If the smaller company could add something that was important to the larger company, the price was worth paying.

Roger Smith decided to try to buy EDS. The employees at EDS would still be doing their work, and Ross Perot would still direct them. But their work would be for GM. GM would pay them and keep EDS's profits.

Everyone who owned EDS stock would profit from such a deal, and Ross was the biggest stockholder. Would he agree to the sale? Could he accept someone telling him what to do in the company he started?

Just as important, how would Ross react to the very different way in which GM operated? It was more formal, more like IBM than EDS.

Ross would become a member of GM's board of directors, the group that had the final say on how the company was run. Could Ross, who now employed 13,000 people at EDS, be happy as part of a huge company with 750,000 workers?

Roger Smith knew that Ross had a different way of working. But he thought his company needed major changes. He wanted Ross to join GM and shake things up. At least he thought he did.

Ross had strong doubts about whether it would work. But Smith told him he liked his style. It was the very thing that had interested GM in EDS. Ross would have a chance to change one of America's industrial giants—and make a lot of money. When GM finally put in writing how EDS could keep its style of working, Ross agreed to the deal.

He signed the contract on his birthday, June 27, 1984. The price GM paid for EDS was $2.5 billion.

A Big Mistake

The combination of EDS and GM turned out to be an almost immediate disaster. As a member of the board of directors, Ross wanted company executives to mix more with employees. He pushed for more direct management. But Roger Smith and other top managers at GM were more comfortable managing at a distance.

GM also went back on its promise to Ross that he could keep managing EDS in his own way. One thing Ross was used to doing was deciding how much to pay each employee. But now GM even insisted on making that decision for him.

The differences continued to mount over the next several months. At one point, Ross sent a note to Smith, telling him that many EDS employees thought that the head of GM was a "bully." Smith did not reply.

It would have been surprising if the two men had been able to merge their different management styles without a clash. Ross Perot had learned about business by starting one from scratch. Roger Smith had gone to business school. Ross was used to making quick decisions, keeping on top of everything, and acting informally. He liked to do things himself. But Smith liked to work slowly, indirectly. He was a careful accountant, most comfortable when working with numbers, not people.

Ross talked to the workers at GM to see what they thought about the company's problems. He visited GM dealers, posing as a customer. While other board members were being driven around in fancy cars, Ross bought an Oldsmobile and drove it himself. When Ross was unhappy about GM, he said so—publicly.

Roger Smith knew how to play by the rules. He was uncomfortable with changing the system. Part of the system was that the board of directors agreed to do whatever he wanted them to do. Ross's vote as a board member was worth little. He could always be outvoted.

Ross and Roger Smith didn't fool each other when GM bought EDS. They were

Ross discussed company policy with workers at a General Motors plant. This style of direct management, although popular with employees, got Ross into trouble with other GM executives.

really fooling themselves. Each man thought he could get the other to be more like himself. But it wasn't going to happen.

When Smith wanted GM's accountants to check EDS's business records in Dallas, Ross wouldn't even let them past the front gate. The very idea of it made Ross feel as if his independence was being limited. But this was how big companies did things.

Clearly, Ross did not fit in at GM. How was the company to get rid of him? The board of directors solved the problem in the way they were used to—with money. They voted to pay Ross about $700 million to leave. This also cut the ties between Ross and EDS, which remained part of GM.

Years later, some people would criticize Ross for taking the money and going. Why did he "quit" when he had set out to change GM? His answer was that he couldn't stay. He was getting nowhere and wasting his time and energy.

Here We Go Again!

As part of the deal, Ross had to agree not to start another company that would compete with EDS for a certain amount of time. He also had to promise not to criticize GM publicly.

But Ross could not hold back and he criticized the car company almost immediately. He scolded them for paying him so much money to leave when they should have applied it to building GM! When Ross started another computer company, Perot Systems, GM sued him. He was accused of unfairly hiring people from EDS—now owned by GM—to staff his new operation.

Ross had not changed. This was clear from the name he chose for the group set up to raise money for his new company. It was called H.W.G.A., for "Here We Go Again."

In the Public Eye

"He was the 'can-do' man who got things done."

Ross Perot didn't suddenly become famous when he ran for president in 1992. He had been in the news often over the past 20 years. Some of his public activities had to do with politics. Others dealt with foreign affairs.

A Texan in Washington

Ross Perot first got involved in politics in 1968, when he became wealthy from the sale of EDS stock. That year he helped Richard Nixon in his campaign for the presidency. When Nixon won, Ross, with money to spend, decided he would offer his services to the new president. For a while nothing came of it.

But thinking that Ross's help might come in handy, President Nixon went out of his way to stay friendly with him. When Ross's company, EDS, ran into some problems in Texas and California, Nixon's staff helped to smooth them out.

Eventually, Nixon did ask Ross for a favor. A big stockbroker in New York was in trouble. If the company failed, there might be a financial panic. Ross's efforts to rescue the company cost him millions of dollars. It was not one of his great successes.

In 1970, when the value of stock dropped, Ross lost much more. His EDS stock declined by $500 million in one day. It was the biggest loss any one person had ever had on a single day on Wall Street.

Ross regained part of his loss by getting several members of Congress to help pass a bill that gave him a special tax break. They pushed it through late at night and made it part of another bill so that few members of Congress would notice it.

To this day, Ross does not like to talk about it. It hardly seems to represent the kind of direct, honest, open way of doing things that he often brags is his style. This kind of deal would come back to haunt him more than once in the future.

A Hero

In 1978, Ross was involved in an incident that made him famous—and a hero.

Two EDS employees had gone to Iran to discuss a contract with the government. When revolution broke out there, they were arrested. After formal talks failed to release the men, Ross took things into his own hands.

He assembled a team of highly trained personnel to rescue the prisoners. Leading the team was Arthur "Bull" Simons, a former officer in the Green Berets—U.S. Army Special Forces—who was trained in guerilla warfare. The whole thing was very dangerous and illegal. Ross went to Iran to visit the imprisoned men first. True to his nature, he was taking another gamble—this time, a very big one.

Fortunately, the assault on the prison proved unnecessary. Before Ross's team was able to make its move, an Iranian EDS employee started a riot that freed the EDS men along with many other prisoners. Questions still remain over whether or not Ross and Bull Simons had anything to do with the riot. Regardless, however, Ross showed amazing courage and determination in his fight to rescue his employees.

In 1978, Ross tried to free two EDS employees from an Iranian jail. Before his rescue team moved in, Ross went to Iran alone to meet with the imprisoned men.

A television mini-series was made about the rescue mission. And Ross Perot became a national legend. He was the "can-do" man who got things done.

Ross Helps Texas

Texas governor William P. Clements was the next to take advantage of Ross Perot's many talents. He made him chief of the state's War on Drugs. Ross dived into the problem. He taught himself what he didn't know, and paid others to gather information for him. The result was a new, tougher and more effective drug law.

Ross followed this with a similar look at education in Texas. He even took on the state's powerful athletic coaches. Ross called for higher academic standards for high school athletes and higher pay for good teachers. He got both.

POWs and MIAs

When he worked with the government, Ross ran into the usual problems. He often seemed to have trouble dealing with people who did not agree with him.

During the Vietnam War, Ross voiced outrage at the number of Americans being held as North Vietnamese prisoners. These were the prisoners of war, or POWs.

Ross decided to take direct action. In late 1969, he chartered a plane filled with food, letters from home, and Christmas presents. He said he was going to take it directly to North Vietnam.

In fact, North Vietnam had already said no. But Ross wanted to make them look bad and perhaps force them to improve their treatment of prisoners. The plane flew to Laos, a country next to North Vietnam. There, Ross was given more directions about repacking everything and shipping it through Moscow to get it to the POWs.

When Ross and a group of volunteers did this, the shipment was refused anyway.

But Ross's message got through, even if the plane didn't. The North Vietnamese and their Russian allies were not as kind as they made themselves out to be. Ross single-handedly outsmarted them. Once again, he was famous.

Ross did not let the issue die. Secretly, he stayed in contact with the North Vietnamese, trying to keep tabs on the POWs. After the war ended in 1975 and the POWs came home, he devoted himself to a new

In late 1969, Ross personally chartered a plane to bring supplies, letters, and Christmas presents to the prisoners of war who were left in Vietnam.

cause. He tried to find out exactly what had happened to soldiers missing in action—MIAs. He set up his own private network of people to gather information. It was almost as if he were running his own foreign policy program.

By the 1980s, many people felt that there were still some POWs left in North Vietnam and perhaps Laos. There had also been reports that MIAs had been spotted alive in these countries. Vice-President George Bush asked Ross to look into the matter in 1986.

What happened after this continues to be in dispute. Ross Perot told George Bush that in digging for information, he kept running into drugs and arms deals involving the U.S. government's spying operations. Eventually, Bush closed the sources of information that Ross had been using. Ross felt that after all his work he was simply being told to forget it.

Ross was not a man to accept such a rejection lightly, especially when he felt that he was going out of his way to help. It left him with bad feelings about George Bush. In 1992, these feelings would play a role on the most public stage of all—the campaign for the presidency.

5

The Biggest Job of All

"What we need is people to stop talking and start doing."

In 1992, Ross Perot turned his attention to his biggest "rescue" mission yet. Ross said that there was a "mess" in Washington. And the increasing national debt upset him most of all. He decided that the way to fix things was to take direct action and go right to the top. He would run for president.

The "Unofficial" Candidate

In the winter of 1992, as voters began to pick the Democratic and Republican candidates for president, one thing was clear: Americans were unhappy with the choices. Neither President Bush nor the Democratic front-runner, Bill Clinton, inspired them.

Ross felt the same way. In February, he appeared on the "Larry King Live" cable television show. As the two men talked about the nation's problems, Larry asked almost casually if the Texan would consider running for president. Ross said he would, but only if the people asked him to do it and if they got his name on the ballot in all 50 states.

This was not an easy task. It involved gathering the signatures of thousands of registered voters in every state. Ross would need an army of volunteers.

He got his army. So many people were fed up with government that Ross's plain

Ross fires up a crowd of about 6,000 supporters at a summer rally in Olympia, Washington, in 1992.

talk and call for action to end the budget problems brought out the volunteers. But were they all volunteers? Ross said they were. Others weren't so sure. Some reports said that Ross Perot was spending money to help "create" this wave of support. By April, that amount was said to be at least $400,000.

As the major-party primaries went on into the spring, the campaign to get Ross on the ballot progressed steadily. Gradually, public-opinion polls began to reflect all the attention Ross was getting in the media. In some polls he was actually running ahead of Democrats and Republicans.

Ross had another thing on his side besides the public unhappiness with "politics as usual." He had money. The U.S. government controlled how much money presidential candidates could spend. In return, it matched the money candidates raised on their own up to a specific limit.

There was, however, a way to get around this spending limit. A candidate who was willing to do without these "matching funds" could spend any amount of money. Ross might have been the only person in America who could afford to do this. If necessary, he said he would spend $100 million of his own money to get elected.

The Problems Begin

Ross had not actually said that he was running. But he was certainly acting like a candidate and was being treated like one. That's when his problems began.

The media will press anyone running for president to say exactly what he or she will do in office. This is especially true when polls show that a candidate might get elected, as Ross's polls did by early summer. The people, after all, have a right to know what they're getting with their vote.

Still an undeclared candidate, Ross greets friends and followers at the opening of his Washington, D.C., campaign headquarters on May 28, 1992.

But Ross was not willing to say exactly what he would do as president. Basically, he said that he would run the government the way he ran his business. He would deal with problems by gathering together all the experts to come up with solutions. He would also conduct "electronic town halls," having people vote on every issue through devices on their television sets. This was his way of giving the customer what he or she wanted. But was it government?

In early May, Ross was having to deal with policy questions constantly. He decided to take some time off from appearing in public so that he might study the issues.

Meanwhile, reporters dug into Ross's past, as they did with all candidates. Some things they turned up were disturbing. For example, there were accusations—never proved—that EDS had overcharged the government on its contracts. Ross was even accused of using his contacts with the North Vietnamese to help his business.

It also came out that Ross had used lie detectors at EDS to see if his employees were honest. He wouldn't let men grow beards. In addition, he favored married white men over single men, women, and other minorities.

As they made the rounds on the campaign trail, Ross and his wife, Margot, stopped to talk with supporters at a rally in Hartford, Connecticut.

His military career was examined. Did he try to have his wealthy, influential father get him out of the navy? Did his family use its influence in government to get an airport built near land they owned, thus increasing its value? Was it true that Ross had hired private investigators to look into the business dealings of President Bush's sons?

The New York Times even reported that Ross had hired investigators to follow his own children. Later, it discovered that he had also investigated his own campaign workers.

On July 16, 1992, Ross announced his decision not to run in the upcoming presidential election. Many followers were confused and disappointed after hearing the news.

By June, the criticism that he called "Mickey Mouse tossed salad" was getting to Ross. He denied everything and blamed it on "Republican dirty tricks" and the media.

A remark about not wanting gays (homosexuals) in his cabinet got Ross into more trouble. And, in a July speech to a civil rights group, Ross referred to blacks as "you people." This insulted his audience.

Finally, on July 16, the day that Bill Clinton accepted his party's nomination, Ross surprised everyone by deciding not to run. He said he was dropping out because his candidacy might prevent anyone from getting the 270 electoral votes needed for victory. This would throw the election into the House of Representatives. And that would not be good for the country.

Many of his supporters were bitter. They had been working hard to get him on the ballot. Some felt that they had backed a quitter.

Ross Returns

But Ross had not yet quit public life. He hired economists to come up with a plan to handle the nation's budget problems. The plan called for higher taxes and decreased spending. It was designed to get the budget balanced by the mid-1990s. He published it as a book entitled *United We Stand: How We Can Take Back Our Country*. Balancing the budget this quickly would have hurt many Americans. Yet the plan was well received as a serious attempt to deal with the nation's problems.

Ross also urged his supporters to keep working to put him on the ballot in every state. This way, Americans who didn't like either Bush or Clinton could cast a protest vote for Ross.

But by late September, Ross was hinting that this might not be enough. Was he thinking of getting back into the race? "If the volunteers said 'It's a dirty job, but you've got to do it,' I belong to them," he told a television interviewer.

On October 1, Ross rejoined the race. But now he was far behind. He had the support of only 10 percent of the voters in the polls. Could he once again become an important part of the campaign?

An Opportunity Seized

When the three presidential candidates, George Bush, Bill Clinton, and Ross Perot met to debate on television, the door was opened for Ross to regain the spotlight. Bush and Clinton had to be careful not to anger Ross's supporters, whose vote might make the difference in a close race. But Ross had nothing to lose. He could attack both men.

Even more important, Ross's style was made to order for the debates. While the other candidates spoke carefully, he fired away with blunt talk and folksy humor.

ROSS PEROT ★ 43

Ross rejoined the 1992 presidential race on October 1. By this time, polls showed that Ross had about 10 percent of the popular vote.

With little hope of actually winning, he didn't have to be too specific. He could just echo the general disgust voters had for the way the system was working.

"I'm just a businessman," not a politician, Ross said. "I am results-oriented, I am action-oriented," he reminded the audience. "What we need is people to stop talking and start doing." He even joked about his big ears to show that he had a sense of humor.

Ross began to spend about 60 million dollars just on television ads. Unlike the usual 30-second ads that were filled with slogans and attacks, his were 30 minutes long. In some, he lectured about America's economic problems with charts and graphs. It was so different that people liked it.

The debates and the ads doubled Ross's support in the polls to 20 percent. It might have gone even higher if he hadn't stumbled in the last week. He suddenly claimed that it was "Republican dirty tricks" that had made him drop out of the race in July. He told a strange story, with no proof, about a Republican attempt to spoil his daughter's wedding with embarrassing photographs. The Republicans called Ross "loony." And the candidate wasted several days of campaigning while he dealt with the issue.

Ross stands with his opponents—George Bush and Bill Clinton—during the second presidential debate of 1992.

A Force to Be Reckoned With

Although Ross did not win even one state on election day, he did get 19 percent of the popular vote. This was the second best showing for an independent candidate in this century.

We will never know how Ross might have done if he had not dropped out of the race in July. Nor is it clear what lies ahead for the self-starter. Without comment, he held up a "Perot '96" sticker as he spoke to his followers on election night. Was the business leader from Texarkana sensing another opportunity down the road? We will have to wait and see.

Glossary

automation The use of devices, such as computers, to replace the work of people.

Green Berets U.S. Army Special Forces whose troops are trained in guerilla warfare.

MIA A person who is missing in action as the result of having fought in a war.

POW A prisoner of war.

primaries Preliminary elections in which voters nominate a candidate for office.

software Instructions, or programs, that are executed by a computer.

stock Ownership in a company that the public acquires by buying shares in it.

For Further Reading

Brown, Gene. *The 1992 Election*. Brookfield, CT: Millbrook, 1992.

Dunnan, Nancy. *Entrepreneurship*. Morristown, NJ: Silver Burdett Press, 1990.

Rockwell, Thomas. *How to Get Fabulously Rich*. New York: Franklin Watts, 1990.

Stewart, Gail. *Texans*. Vero Beach, FL: Rourke Corporation, 1990.

Index

Abortion, 6
Annapolis, Maryland, 9, 11

Birmingham, Margot (wife), 10, 43
Blue Cross–Blue Shield, 16
Boy Scouts of America, 8
Bush, George, 6, 33, 34, 39, 42, 45

Clements, William P., 30
Clinton, Bill, 34, 41, 42, 45
Congress, U.S., 16, 28

Education reform, 31
Electronic Data Systems (EDS), 15, 16–17, 22, 28, 38
  association with General Motors, 20, 22–26
  Iran hostage situation, 29–30
  stock, 17, 27, 28

"**F**amily values," 6

General Motors (GM), 20, 21, 23, 24
  association with Electronic Data Systems, 20, 22–23, 24–26
Green Berets (U.S. Army Special Forces), 29

International Business Machines (IBM), 11, 12–13, 14, 15, 19
Iran, 29–30
Iraq, 6

Korean War, 10

"**L**arry King Live," 35
Leyte (ship), 11

Medicaid, 16
Medicare, 16
MIAs, 33

Naval Academy, U.S., 9–10, 11

Navy, U.S., 10, 11, 12, 39
Nixon, Richard, 27, 28

Patterson, Mary, 8
Perot, Gabriel Ross (father), 7, 8
Perot, H. Ross
  birth, 7
  childhood, 7–9
  marriage, 10, 12
  1992 campaign for U.S. presidency, 5–6, 27, 33, 34–45
  wealth, 18
Perot, Lulu Ray (mother), 7–8
Perot Systems, 26
Persian Gulf War, 6

POWs, 31–33
Presidential debates (1992), 42, 44, 45

Simons, Arthur "Bull," 29
Smith, Roger, 21, 22, 24–25

Texarkana, Texas, 7, 8–9
Texarkana Junior College, 9

United We Stand: How We Can Take Back Our Country, 41

Vietnam War, 31–32, 33, 38

War on Drugs, 30

Photo Credits:
Cover: ©Kennedy/Gamma Liaison; p. 4: ©David Woo/Gamma Liaison; p. 10: ©Woo/Gamma Liaison; p. 11: ©Woo/Gamma Liaison; p. 17: AP/Wide World Photos; p. 21: Wide World Photos; p. 35: Wide World Photos; p. 37: Wide World Photos; p. 39: ©P. Gifford/Gamma Liaison; p. 40: Wide World Photos; p. 43: ©Woo/Dallas Morning News/Gamma Liaison; p. 45: ©Dick Halstead/Gamma Liaison.

Illustrations by Jerry Harston.